# Original Ruse

POEMS

Barbara Sabol

Accents Publishing
Lexington, KY
WINGED SERIES

Copyright © 2011 by Barbara Sabol
All rights reserved

Printed in the United States of America

**Accents Publishing Winged Series**
Editor: Katerina Stoykova-Klemer
Artist: Simeon Kondev

Accents Publishing is an independent press for brilliant voices. For a catalog of current and upcoming titles, please visit us on the Web at
http://www.accents-publishing.com

The Winged Series features selections from Accents Publishing Poetry Chapbook contests.

ISBN: 978-0-9844118-7-0
First Edition
10 9 8 7 6 5 4 3 2 1

*for Tom*

# Table of Contents

Original Ruse ..................................................................... 1
*Vermis* Equinox .................................................................. 3
Poem with a First Line from a Fragment by Sappho ................... 4
To the Grocery List ............................................................. 5
Convection Theories ............................................................ 6
Triboluminescence at 12 ....................................................... 7
Peaches .............................................................................. 8
Bounty ............................................................................... 9
Daydreamer ...................................................................... 10
Over-Easy at the All-Night Diner ......................................... 11
First Date or Ways to Fix Zucchini ....................................... 12
Post Card, Orleans Bay ....................................................... 13
Waiting in Line with a Loaf of Wonder Bread, I Glance at *Star* ..... 14
Winter .............................................................................. 15
Husbandry ........................................................................ 16
The Prickly Pear's Careful Inquiry ....................................... 17
Wedlock ........................................................................... 18
When the Blue-Hatted Muse Speaks .................................... 19
To the Vocal Cords ............................................................ 20
Broach .............................................................................. 21
Refuge .............................................................................. 22
Imagine a Town ................................................................. 23
At the Loneliness Convention ............................................. 24
Escape Artists at the Movies ............................................... 25
On Considering the Purchase of a New Mattress ................... 26
Hell and Gone ................................................................... 27
*Poseur* ............................................................................ 28
Hula Girls ......................................................................... 29
Happiness ......................................................................... 30

*Climbing away
from heaven ~
ant in a sugar bowl*

# Original Ruse

*i*

No apple was worth the risk, not even
an Asian pear apple, the snappish bite
and comely shape, like a sister.
(Besides she had no map to locate Japan,
no dictionary to look up *exotic*.)

Even a Gala, succulent as a cool-
tongued French kiss, was better left
to glow pinkly on that one cordoned-off tree.
(There was that problem of a map, and
no produce catalog.)

Bored by his puny repertoire of stories, small
store of words to describe the world
(always jabbering: *birds, look, monkeys, funny,
again? perfect, perfect*), she wandered

out past the orchard, to the garden's reaches,
only seeking quiet, space to consider
the real meaning of perfection.
(Convenient, the lack of a dictionary.)

But he was always after her, a constant
annoyance. You can imagine. She longed to
drink her coffee in peace, an occasional morning.
It didn't seem like a selfish entreaty.

*ii*

Past the rows of self-tilling beans, yellow melons fattening
in the heat, the flowers she knew from their odor (naming them
herself – orchid, narcissus, skunk cabbage),
                              she discovered something new:

She knew the genus instinctively: Nightshade, lovely word.
She also fathomed that plants in this family could be toxic.
But that fragrance – perfumed dirt, musky green,
summer-downpour-heat-lightning pungent –
$$\text{irresistible.}$$

And it fell so easily from the vine.


*iii*

He had followed her there, found her
warming this blood-red globe in her palm.
He watched as she pressed her nose to the stem,
breathed it in with a kind of rapture
he'd never witnessed.

So, after a small bite, just a nick
in the soft skin, after coddling it
against her palate, then grabbing the nearest limb
for balance, she had no choice
but to hand it over.

## *Vermis* Equinox

It's not air or escape
from saturated digs,
so much as the impulse
toward creation that lures
the earthworm back above
ground – the flaccid grass slick
as a just-born, under
the last few shards of snow.
Worth risking the robin's
beak, the groundhog's grubby
clutch, is the writhe along
the length of its see-through
segments, each link purpose-
driven: one to burrow,
one to digest, and two
to ooze out a cocoon.
Either way, for breath or
love (blind to the difference),
they shimmy up, powered
by five miniscule hearts.
Each muscled ring a clause
dependent on the next:
God's first articulate
terrestrial sentence.

# Poem with a First Line from a Fragment by Sappho

No more than the bird with piercing voice,
    this sweep of light across the grass. Evening
        quickens. The wood thrush calls down
            the last plumes of violet, bruising the
                      air

beneath – the familiar double-warbled cry. Though much
    is understood about the bending of light, passing
        through one medium (say, dimming day) to
            another of less velocity (say, a glass,
                      water)

how is it the light, along with the bird and its sorrow song,
    bows, if you will, along some vector, an angling of $x$
        toward a denser $y$, so that what we perceive
            shifts as we look, slant as a fault in the
                      earth.

Nothing truer than my palm curving the shape of your thirst
    and its quenching, as I carry a glass of tap water,
        brimming, out through the twilit yard, to where
            you sit aslant the purpling
                      sky.

Everything, even the water in its amber tumbler, all
    its immaculate droplets intact, stills and is held by this
        tapering half-light, by the pitch of a half-recalled
            call, response; the glass, our hands
                      vanishing

## To the Grocery List

This incantation
of greens and grains,
rosy citrus in season
appeases with textures
and odors rising
from scrap paper.
Add the alchemists: butter,
flour – subtleties
of roux: scant ballast
against earth's slack-jawed
hunger – splitting like
overleavened bread,
and the sea spills
from its immense bowl,
salting the land. What
can the hands do
but knead and blend.
The fingers themselves
marvel, and the tongue
in every living
language weeps.

# Convection Theories

Before the storm, anything
but calm – wind catches
the private undersides of oak leaves,
holds them up to the elements,
and then with that first crack
of thunder I am running
to unplug appliances large and small,
checking ghost currents that might set us –
you, me, the dogs, the end tables – alight.

Last month a storm like this
sent a pin oak crashing
right through my neighbor's roof
into the front and back bedrooms.
It was early evening, thank God,
and they were downstairs,
just finishing dinner.

Somehow the whole family managed
to walk out the front door,
survey the wreckage
of their wooden house, mangled
as a sea-tossed ship, and like
spared survivors of disaster,
stand linked together on the sidewalk,
repeating to their unscathed neighbors,
*How lucky we were, how blessed.*

So quick, that spear of light, the heart-
splitting howl of opposites in motion.
Then the release of a cooling downburst.
Here we flip the switches back on,
                              breathe.

If only our inevitable fights could work like this –
the wild whip of words, our tendernesses
exposed, then the generous abandon
of rain.

## Triboluminescence at 12

Bowed alone into the intentional dark
of my bedroom closet to forge a spark,
I crouch among denim, walking shoes –
animal odors of back and forth woes.
Playground talk's more than rude fiction
with all my extremities craving friction,
while my tongue retraces the raised details
on a hard white ring, innocent lingual Braille:
Wint-O-Green – Oh the visceral anticipation
as my teeth scout out the willing section
and bite. Electrons rogue from the atom
toward new unions till now unfathomed:
molecules meet mid-air, an ultraviolet
encounter; and I, for one potent moment
glow: a quick, blue cloud marks the union
of self and charged self, some chemistry proven.
One milk-molared gesture tokens the possible –
a cool ghostly host, mouthed into the miracle
of body coursing blood, a newly minted wonder
as this first flinted lightning gives way to thunder.

# Peaches

Give me the savor
of those summer peaches,
the ones Mom crossed two lanes for
in rush hour, swerving
into Hartman's produce stand,
which appeared every June,
transforming the gravel lot
at Bailey and State
into a succulent mirage.

Orbits so full
they filled my entire hand
like a softball.

Frankie and I scrabbled
into the brown paper bag
right there in the dusty lot.
Our mouths so swamped
with pleasure, it curled
our toes in our sneakers.
We couldn't even look
at each other as we slurped
and gulped the wet pulp.

The best we could manage was
a startled moan when she called us
to get on back in the car.

# Bounty

We bought sacks of grapes and figs,
ham sweating fat from the island store –
too much, perhaps, for two people
and a week, handing our exotic coins
to the man with the blood-smeared apron
and Brutus forearms. Full of the sun's
brazen light, we outroared the waves,
your white shirt flapping about your hips,
as up and back we strolled the beach
by the rope-muscled boy tossing chum
to greedy gulls, and felt fine shells
crackling under our soles. He looked away
when we passed him. At night we'd soak
in the tepid pool, cracked along its oval length
like a grin. And after gorging on salty cheese,
plump olives, thick stew rinsed with wine, after
our skin swelled with each other, we'd polish
limbs and backs with virgin oils and sleep
greased on sheets as thick as sails. Our dreams
crowded with a stumbling of hooves.

# Daydreamer

> *So many people come into a picture, posing for parts of bodies... Andy's always fiction.*
> - Betsy Wyeth

Lifting arms overhead, I pull off my blouse
and resume an upright pose – becoming instead
his dreaming dancer, spinning, spun toward the bed
under the hooks in the low-ceilinged farmhouse,
by the window framing the river's cascade.
This room's beguiled by the shape of sleep;
my shadow curves around me, a warm beast,
as he gauges angles of daylight and shade.

He sketches me as morning light enters,
donned in other women's skin, others' faces,
though my sovereign vales and interior places
suggest a country his brushes cannot alter,
as I lie wakeful, daydreaming, his pretender –
unfurled like a flag, but not in surrender.

# Over-Easy at the All-Night Diner

I dump out the old brew and sizzle up the grill around dawn,
when the third shifters thin out and the day shift rolls in, then
I spot him; red stitching above his breast pocket reads, *Tom*.

In wrinkled coveralls, he leans on the counter and orders eggs
over hard; yolk hard as the August sun (bubbled like fresh tar
under his roller); leaves me his change and downs the dregs.

Most folks take theirs over-easy. They like for the yolk to ooze,
and sop it up with a slice of bread. Most still dreaming, eyes half-
open; maybe wishing the day was already over, but nobody says.

Bet he knocks off same time as me; I follow him home, in my head:
a tidy one-bedroom painted light blue, with pictures on the walls.
We'd sleep in till whenever, and then I'd bring his eggs to the bed –

over-easy this time, spread jelly on his toast. Then he turns me once,
easy, over. I notice the color of his eyes. (This is where it gets blurry –
we have nothing to say, or say nothing; either way, things get tense.)

I'll keep an eye out for a guy with a sewn-on name, to spoil my theory
while I sizzle up the grill, scoop out fine-ground joe, in no big hurry.

## First Date or Ways to Fix Zucchini

I expected maybe a bouquet – blooms
not weighted with prospect – something
ingenuous like asters or carnations
would have charmed me utterly.

But he handed me a zucchini – anatomically
superlative. *This is for you* (one raised
brow). *Organic. Grew it myself* (gaze
averted). Afterwards, how could I notice

anything else – the color of his eyes, those
elegant fingers, smooth half-moon nail beds,
the smile that had practically breathed fall apples
and Jameson out of his digitized photo?

The taste that lingered, however, was of gruyère,
garden parsley, sweet onion from an excellent
zucchini *au gratin*, which he tasted
without relish, seconds or dessert.

## Post Card, Orleans Bay

The Bay too chill this time of year
for bathing; we sit and watch the skiffs
drift – aimless as the clouds.

This closing day of our idle
journey, under a wide blue umbrella,
we linger in a cordial stupor,

long after a flock of terns, flying south,
pulls the flat sash of evening
across the water.

# Waiting in Line with a Loaf of Wonder Bread, I Glance at *Star*

Fated by a pleasant smile, teeth even
as a new sidewalk, no cracks, broken backs.
Aging Breck Girl with a face perfect
strangers mistake for an old neighbor, the off-
duty checkout girl.

Mostly blond at 52, no ominous checks
on the medical history form. Punctual as a
three-and-a-half minute egg, yolk just right
for dipping. Neat as a cliché, as the denouement
of a dime novel.

Dutiful, I play the pleasant friend; never
the ample heroine glistening with wretchedness.
Tucked behind plain luck, I brace for the squeeze
of a rock – diamond or obsidian – and a uniquely
ruinous place.

# Winter

*Inspired by a fragment from Sappho*

Winter is a country
that settles
in your limbs, stirs
the joints – mortar,
pestle – and your own
weather shivers
against the changes
as it takes up
residence
in the vintage bones.

If not winter,
it's your years
that hush the blood,
cooling
the snow-pebbled skin
as your own
paler season
seeps in
by degrees
with little fuss.

If winter, then
you take it all in –
what choice do you have
but to absorb
the fading, green-
tinged light
like absinthe, color
of forgetting, first
and last
color of the world.

# Husbandry

Deer step out of the thinning woods nightly: hunger
makes them bold, almost tame. They head for his
gentleman's garden in the side yard: experimental
carrots and bib lettuce striking roots.

He bound the brood with woven wire – protection
from motley appetites invading our land. Cursing
with each barb prick, he finished the useless fence in one night,
then, coming back in, grimed the knob with muck and blood.

At dusk I watch as two does approach, their heads a soft angle
to the tentative morsels. They accept the snag and pull of wire
over muzzles, black gums drawing back as they work
the bitter husks of winter tomatoes.

I think the taste must be sweet to them, like living.
*Let them feed. What harm?* But he runs at them and they scatter
into thin suburban wilds. Mornings, a wasted breath
clings like dew to the backs of melons.

Furtive creatures with those eyes viscous black, quick, the deer
snort and stomp just inside the tree line through our edgy sleep.
Would they settle for tufts of bunch grass, forsythia leaves –
small satisfactions – if we just let them in?

## The Prickly Pear's Careful Inquiry

Each thorn a gesture
to the petals' delicacy,
while the yellow bloom
tempers each point
of its stem's menace.

# Wedlock

You say *sedimentary*, guiding me
along the ledges, and point out
alluvial layering, where
hard and soft rocks have folded
over one another across time.

I only notice shadows
of various branches shifting
across mossy boulders
whose faces change from
amusement to chill derision.

## When the Blue-Hatted Muse Speaks

       Like middle-aged lust – inconvenient,
startling – the urge comes fierce.
       Triggered by someone talking
about downing some Red Stripe
at a motel in Lodi or by a blue
pillbox hat in an old *Life*
photo (black and white, but I know
it's blue), complete with netting –
her painted lips mouthing something
I can almost make out.
       Another time by some falling-
down shed in a cornfield, County Road 27,
on a day so hot the cobs roast as they grow.
       Enough to send me, nymph-swift,
shoeless, to my desk, listen
to what the blue-hatted woman
is whispering. She knows the taste
of Ohio sweet corn, dripping
butter, chased by an iced cold
bottle of beer.
       Backlit by flashing neon – *Vacancy:*
She insists *describe it, black on white,*
*my inspired, vivid kiss.*

# To the Vocal Cords

    Crazed cage, undo.                                       Woo
all the wild birds to our room.
Word flurry, we know exactly
how to mean, know our voices,
sensate strings, will carry us,                     quiver us
home.
    Pearly bi-valve, winged
sphincter, elegant bongo, wah wah           mouth,
shake the startled Formica space
between us. Slick confession box,
you clamor then catch;                               breath
suddenly renegade.
    Timid window, you let in                 a sigh,
you sing, stammer, in time
seduce. Our sounds dip and                      glide
across palate and tongue
that suckles speech like nectar
through a stem, by lips that                     Oh
    if he leaned across that
clean space and kissed me,                     what
sounds might keen – ardent as kids
on a roller coaster:   gasp                   snatched
at the crest,         loosed
                        into vertical

                                              oblivion.

# Broach

        Glitter fish,
tarnished star wreath,
with your clasp gone
how will you fasten
to my black cashmere,
tight across the chest
unbuttoned to . . . *yes*
    *oh yes*
he said at the Blue Sky
Drive-In, clinched
against the red leather
of his Corvair convertible.
        How to sparkle now
with your rhinestones half-
slipped? A galaxy of longing
sputters in the night.

# Refuge

> *When you're over with something, you're over*
> *with it... unless it has the flash of the real thing,*
> *I don't want to drag it out.*
>                          – Andrew Wyeth

He came to me with his graphite points, his velum,
and we tramped, one last time, out to the woods

high above the school house, our boots breaking through
crusted snow. This time, he let me wander,

finding my own pose against the old apple tree where once
I leaned away from this orchard – arching skyward

yet tethered. With younger limbs, I'd climb in spring
and stretch out along branches stout as a man's leg.

In another season, he painted me flush in a mound
of fern moss where trunk and ground unite, brush-

stroked my hair, my skin – textured as the rocks,
cloud-hued. With his eyes. I was muscled as this trunk.

Now he is absorbed by other shapes and colors.
The moon and its blinding madness. His back bared

to the wet air. My figure, once his familiar, huddles,
collared against the chill. Eclipsed by this tower

of coarse bark rising to a tangle in the cast-iron sky,
he draws me into its hollowed center.

## Imagine a Town

Imagine a town like Slaughterville
Oklahoma with every citizen all
three thousand some gone grand
poof some ghost towns
aren't inhabited even by ghosts
they don't stick around
for their own haunting
trusting the waterless wind
to bang the shutters no one
left to shudder or slide an arm
around an imaginary back
practically feel the warmth grasp
an absent hand waltzing
around a darkened parlor

# At the Loneliness Convention

The windows in the back room
of Johnnie's Mission Inn
have painted themselves
shut. The door
is a sleepless mattress,
sprung
at head and hip points.
Still, there is air enough
for the moderator's brief
announcements: one
by one, we strain forward
in our wooden folding chairs
to hear his whispery listing
of the day's activities:
– unlimited wandering about the room,
– gazing through double-paned windows,
– Beat the Devil competitions.
Lunch, of course, is on our own.
He hands us each a name badge
which reads:   *Anonymous*
    *Anonymous*    *Anonymous*

## Escape Artists at the Movies

We savor the syncopated repartee
from perfectly bowed lips.
Connoisseurs of the blinding smile,
we watch for foreshadowing
in the vaulted darkness, say *ah ha*
when the scissors she used to trim
anniversary roses hover
above his heart.

They invite what frightens us most –
easy betrayal, the slow simmer, truth.
Afterward, cast back
into our ordinary shoes,
we shuffle between screen
and sedan, united
by the intrigue, the predictable
ending.

At home, I pour wine, undo
a button, shuffle cards at the table
while he shifts in his chair, clears
his throat, turns the page
of a novel.

## On Considering the Purchase of a New Mattress

Back to back we slide into that groove transversing
   the length of our bed long years of carving our
      dreams that glide us to two contented
         bottoms anchoring a V up to our
          pillowed heads drawn by the
           inevitable pull back to
            center shaping a
             little victory
              nightly

# Hell and Gone

I took the roundabout route home from school
to avoid cutting through the underpass
where you are sure to see the tapered toes,
the dingy split leather beyond the trestle.
I can't say we weren't warned: he'd be leaning
against the concrete wall, whistling like a train,
blowing smoke rings, and jostling his crotch
like a pouch of silver, the linen cod piece
rubbed thin. The small of his back tapered
into the clammy concrete. Patient, watching
for a pony-tailed catechist, innocence
creased into the pleats of her blue uniform.

\* \* \*

We held our breath and pedaled better than wind
past the House of Death: smashed-in windows,
wood-rot porch, the decadent lean of abandonment
over Torchia's hill. We believed that to inhale
its corruption was our peril. Short years later,
our pleasure: rocking under the awkward weight
of some Jimmy, I splintered my teenaged ass
on its parched floorboards in plain daylight.
                              Calling it, *tails*.

\* \* \*

Post beams still hunch over that hill, stubborn
as lust, will. Now when I walk past with my dogs,
their flagship tails high in the October brightness,
a rustle of oak leaves falls, falls back to earth.

## *Poseur*

One would expect feathers
puffing from sleeves or
incandescent gestures
(voices weak
from disuse).

But it's the shoes
that give them away –
the clopping gait. See
how the feet bulge
in their leather housing.

Someone hobbling
with just one shoe (like
an old sneaker) is probably
an angel: the mate left
on some roadside or beach.

Metal shavings may tangle
in the crown of her hair.
At dusk, when the light
angles just so, they appear
to sparkle there.

Watch for them at cafés.
An angel usually orders espresso,
knocks it back in one swig.
She may thumb through a magazine,
distracted. Waiting for someone

to join her at the corner table;
someone whose features are known
by description alone. Check out
her feet – tapping, tapping.
So much to do.

## Hula Girls

The saleswoman assured me it was fashionable, revealing
just a hint of thigh, white as twice-whipped potatoes.
I chose the gaudiest of the bunch: yolk yellow

with red piping – wanting to be visible while concealed
this maiden summer of my leisure years. The skirt wafts
above my waist – brazen manta flashing

like the Hula Girl hibiscus bushes Mother and I had planted
each spring: we'd tamped the soil with vermiculite,
staining our fingers with creaturely smells of dark

appetite, tasting bits of mica in our sleep. All summer,
I had pinched out the stem tips so the showy flowers
with their ruby eyes could bloom continuously.

The clerk also held out a black, one-piece suit,
material thick and shiny as seal skin
with a diagonal design meant to trick the eye.

In my two-piece job, I bob into the current, toes curling
in the lake-bottom ooze, my hair silvers the water,
a flowering crown.

# Happiness

The mouth
of the vase
is not calling out

for asters
for water
its cobalt glass

curves
around the notion
of flowers

a quenched stem
and window light
scattering

the blueness